THE 5 STAGES OF HEARTBREAK

The 5 Stages of Heartbreak

BECCA GREENBERG

Becca Greenberg

to everyone who ever broke my heart
and those who helped fix it

Content Warning

This book contains sensitive topics that might be uncomfortable for some readers. Please observe the list below for potentially upsetting content.

Drug and Alcohol Abuse
Emotional and Physical Abuse
Sexual Abuse
Self Injury
Suicide and Suicidal Ideation

Contents

denial   1

anger   27

bargaining   53

depression   79

acceptance   107

denial

fog

i had a plan. i had a set way our life would go.
nothing could get in the way of what i dreamt about.
and yet, there you were. creating such a disturbance
that fogged up my vision, till i had no choice but to let go.
much like fog though, it doesn't feel real. after all,
how can so many little things cover your entire
world so quickly? so strongly?

questions

you didn't have to do that you know.
i was on cloud nine. i was flying, i was free.
you didn't have to cut the rope.
you didn't have to leave me stranded, falling
towards earth.
i didn't want to believe that you did what you did to me.
even as i lay broken on the ground,
covered in unanswerable questions,
i still held onto the rope you'd cut.

gainsay

you always had my hand wrapped around yours.
"why are you staring at that guy? flirting
right in front of me?"
i hadn't slept with anyone else in over a year.
"you're such a fucking whore."
tears had coated my eyes as you slipped the ring
onto my finger.
"good luck finding someone else, no one
will ever love you as much as i do."
i helped pick out baby names and search for
apartments with you.
"done. over. go cry if you want but i doubt
you actually will."

investigating

maybe it was in the flowers you sent me.
       but i pulled off all the petals and only saw a stem.
maybe you hid it in the hoodies you gave me.
         but there was no loose threads to pull apart.
maybe it was in the love notes you sent me.
          but there was no code to be decrypted.
i searched, and searched, and searched.
even now i still look for an explanation.
you had to hurt me, you had to leave me.
             but why?

rejection

i gave you my love. i gave you gifts. i gave you my time.
you can't just throw it away like that.
can you?

disavowal

you can't do that. you couldn't of.
you don't get to break me and walk away without pain.
you don't get to ruin me, ruin us.
                                        but you did.
                            and you made it my fault.
        because you couldn't bear the responsibility of your
                                                actions.
        you couldn't admit that you were the one to ruin it.

trial

maybe this is all a test. maybe you're running away
to see what i'll do. to see my love, pure and raw.
maybe you'll come back and tell me not to worry.
maybe you'll tell me you never meant those words
you said. maybe, maybe, maybe.
maybe you didn't have to test me in the first place.

torrential

there wasn't a way to divert the flood. the way you
broke my heart shattered me. it sent my body down
a river to be pelted by an endless torrential stream
of hurt. yet i still convinced myself i was okay
because the pieces of my body were still floating.

confliction

why? why do you do this? i'll never understand.
hey, there's no need to be sorry, i understand.
all i do is try endlessly, but it's never enough.
why do you make me hate myself?
you have your feelings for a reason,
i get it if i made it worse.
i've already given you my all, i can't give you
something from nothing.
i'm sorry that i'm not enough for you,
though i'm trying to be.
i'm so done with this but i don't know how to leave.
i don't know how to give up.
i don't want this to be over. please,
let me go,
don't leave me.
i love you.
atleast i think i did.

why

why. *why.* why. *why.* why. *why.* why. *why.* why. *why.* why.
why. why. *why.* why. *why.* why. *why.* why. *why.* why. *why.*
why. *why.* why. *why.* why. *why.* why. why. *why.* why. *why.*
why. *why.* why. *why.* why. *why.* why. *why.* why. *why.* why.
why. *why.* why. *why.* why. *why.* why. *why.* why. *why.* why.
why. why. *why.* why. why. *why.* why. *why.* why. *why.* why.
why. why. *why.* why. *why.* why. *why.* why. why. *why.* why.
why. why. *why.* why. *why.* why. *why.* why. *why.* why. *why.*
why. why. *why.* why. *why.* why. *why.* why. *why.* why. *why.*
why. *why.* why. *why.* why. why. *why.* why. *why.* why. *why.*
why. *why.* why. *why.* why. *why.* why. *why.* why. why. *why.*
why. *why.* why. *why.* why. *why.* why. *why.* why. *why.* why.
why. why. why. *why.* why. *why.* why. *why.* why. *why.* why.
why. why. *why.* why. *why.* why. why. *why.* why. *why.* why.
why. why. *why.* why. *why.* why. *why.* why. *why.* why. why.
why. why. *why.* why. *why.* why. *why.* why. *why.* why. *why.*
why. *why.* why. why. *why.* why. *why.* why. *why.* why. *why.*
why. *why.* why. *why.* why. *why.* why. why. *why.* why. *why.*
why. *why.* why. *why.* why. *why.* why. *why.* why. *why.* why.
why. *why.* why. *why.* why. *why.* why. *why.* why. *why.* why.
why. why. *why.* why. why. *why.* why. *why.* why. *why.* why.
why. why. *why.* why. *why.* why. *why.* why. why. *why.* why.
why. why. *why.* why. *why.* why. *why.* why. *why.* why. *why.*
why. why. *why.* why. *why.* why. *why.* why. *why.* why. *why.*
why. *why.* why. *why.* why. why. *why.* why. *why.* why. *why.*
why. *why.* why. *why.* why. *why.* why. *why.* why. why. *why.*
why. why. *why.* why.

why?

searching

the gaping hole within me widens with every stroke
of your words which you've welded into a blade.
the strings of my heart sing like a breaking violin as
your bow is made of razors, not love. i could never
explain why you chose to hurt me in the way that
you did. i searched. for days, weeks, months.
searching far and wide for an answer. if someone
who loved you as much as they said they did, they
wouldn't hurt you like this...
would they?

confusion

my idea of love has been skewed since i was a
child. it wasn't my fault, i don't think. life happens
and it happened around me. it happened to me.

consent

i said no
to bacon on the side of my pancakes,
and to having my coffee with creamer.
i said no
to wearing my moms hideous green dress,
and to changing my favorite shoes.
i said no
to going out on that friday night,
and to picking up that extra shift.
i said no
to getting my nails done,
and to cutting my hair above my shoulders.
i said no
to throwing out the flowers he gave me months ago,
and to giving away his hoodies.
i said no
to giving up on my dream,
and to letting their opinions define me.
in all of those scenarios,
and many many more like them,
when i said no,
those around me listened.
their pursuit of their ideas and opinions
were dropped without a second thought.
this to me, elicits the question...
of all those people and their ability to hear my no,
why?
why when i told *him* no,
why didn't he listen?

when

when did you decide to hate me? that you didn't
love me? when did you decide that i was no longer
worth the fight?
was it when i "broke your heart"?
or was it when you held me after we made love and
you told me i was the only girl in the world? was it
when you wrapped your arms around me when i
cried as you wiped my tears away? was it when we
spent all those nights together, laughing at things
only we found funny?
or was it when you kissed me, looked me in the
eyes and told me you loved me?

where

if someone asks me where we first met,
      my cheeks burn red with the memory.
the random circumstance to which we crossed paths,
      the humor of it all.
if someone asked me where we fell in love,
      i'd tell them with a bashful smile,
as i remember the vulnerability of that night
      and the smiles we shared.
but if someone asked me where we drifted apart,
      my brain runs itself dry
trying to decide where you discovered i was no longer
worth it,
      and where your love was spent better off some-
   place else.

avoidance

it's easy to turn a blind eye,
to redirect my tears back into my head.
it's simple, to find a new route to work.
a new path to avoid all the places we dreamt about.
it's painless to change my style.
transform myself into someone else.
but there's no way to avoid the burning in my chest,
from the rips you made in my heart.

denial

there's no way,
the man i once loved,
who i wanted everything with,
could change into someone this cruel.

there is simply no way.

who

i knew who you were when i fell in love with you.
a sweet soul, someone who the world had not been
kind to.
yet you smiled nonetheless.
you were someone who made me believe in myself.
who made me believe in love again,
and taught me what it meant to be truely valued.
that's why i ask,
who were you when you broke my heart?
because the boy i loved wasn't that cruel.
the boy i loved didn't rage at me and made me
doubt my self worth.
the boy i loved didn't make me afraid to love again.
so who was that?

mistrust

i do a lot of things wrong.
like math, i can't do math.
i struggle to understand the equations
and how they all have an answer.
i don't get advanced math,
and frankly i hate trigonometry.
like how multiple sides to one shape,
all are different.
yet if they're all different,
how are they still the same shape?
but i thought,
there's no way something as simple as a line
could ever have more sides than one.
but here you've proved me wrong yet again.
        except instead of shapes, you showed me all the
                    different sides of you.

requiem

i miss our talks.
our late night conversations and quiet smiles.
i miss our bond.
how our love could exist outside of the bed, not only in it.
i miss your heart.
and the way it provided me a future filled with love.
but i mostly miss who you pretended to be.
as someone as vile as you became,
you made me miss things that weren't even true.

pills

take two capsules.
once a day, with a meal.
watch out for the side effects.
they'll make you sit in the good times,
convince you that the love is still there,
that the person you loved is still who you fell in love with.

what

what was i missing?
we were near perfect.
i had all the important dates written in my notebook,
i talked to your family about how much i adored you,
we went on dates and looked at each other in awe.
so what did i overlook when you left me?
what did i forget?
what was i missing?

invalid

you used to yell at me for faking what i was feeling
when you didn't believe the reason why i felt the
way i felt. as though my emotions themselves
were misdirected. you told me that i didn't love
you. that i didn't care for you. you wrote out your
own script for me to read from and no amount of
truth telling i could give, could ever convince
you i wasn't doing anything but merely improvising.

glass

i used to think my heart was carved from stone.
strong, resilient, powerful.
yet it only took loving you to show me that my
heart was in fact, glass.
easily broken and forever shattered.

anger

rush

i fell in love with you faster than i care to admit.
but you slipped from my grasp even faster,
and had me burning my hands, trying to catch the
fleeting embers you left.

cut

i trace parts of my body with a sharpie,
grabbing at the scissors in an attempt to cut off
the places i've marked.
maybe if they didn't exist,
maybe if i looked more like *them*,
maybe then someone would love me,
and only me.

agony

i hate how much i still love you.
how after i found out every
"i love you"
"it's us forever"
"you and only you"
- was a lie.

i hate how i still wanted you.

elicit

you draw out the darkest parts of me. the parts of
my soul that are corrupt and vile. i convice myself
it's still love, even though i no longer know who
you fell in love with.

burn

our world went up in flames.
and i ran around, throwing buckets of water.
trying to extinguish the flames.
but i caught a glimpse of you,
laughing on the sidelines.
and only then did i notice you holding a burning match.

abuse

i remember standing in the kitchen, tears streaming down my face as i argued with my dad. begging and pleading that you did love me. i was fighting to prove to him that you were good, while simultaneously fighting to hide the bruises you gave me the night before.

i convinced myself that that was love.

anger

i used to think red, hot, sweltering rage would consume me if i ever found out my lover loved another. and maybe i did. maybe i felt it in the beginning. but when everyone you've ever loved has chosen someone else, the rage simmers to a dull pain. one that eggs you on to be mad, to feel anger and hatred. but i am simply too tired to hate, even though i know i should.

blade

i imagine what it would feel like to rip your heart to
shreds.
to take it from your body and stomp it into the ground.
how you'd look after i destroyed every piece of you.

maybe then you'd know how i felt.

heat

there was nothing i could do to prevent your actions.
it was never my fault,
yet you made it out to be,
since you left me with no other explanation.

sweat

i work myself to the bone.
blood, sweat, and tears.
those were the ingredients that made up my love for you.
you pushed me more than anyone ever had.
and i stayed- i *fought*.
but i guess my effort clouded my vision.
and you slipped away from me even when i was still
fighting.
i didn't even notice you left.

hunger

you consumed me like a man starved.
you took my heart and ate it whole.
and i sat and watched.
plastered my face with a fake smile,
and convinced myself the rage in your eyes was love-
not just an evil hunger.

rage

sometimes,
i wish i never fucking met you.
harsh? yes.
but my life was left in shambles since you came.
you destroyed me.

agitate

i sit there, seething in your lies. to play the game of
"who hurt who more." i don't speak. i don't respond.
but in my head i guarantee i already made you cry.
how dare you accuse me of being a liar yet look
me in my eyes and do the same? you sit there,
agitating me, pining for a reaction. but i've learned.
shut up and take it. you'll realize soon the extent
to which you pushed me when i am no longer able
to control my hurt.

i pray for you when that moment comes.

torment

you torment me with the happiness you have when i'm
not around.
     why can't i make you feel like that?
you dangle threats above my head to get me to behave.
     why must you be so violent?
you strip me down to nothing with the harshness of
your words.
     why can't you be kind?
you scare me, turning my body black and blue.
     why can't i just be held by you?

disposable

sometimes,
i think if i couldn't feel my heartbeat,
i wouldn't know that i was human.
because i am treated as though i am to be used,
then thrown away.

control

your words, like knives, have cut me to the bone. i look
unto the mirror and see your insults, your
accusations, your *hate,* scrawled across my body.
marks covering the places i've grown to hate, simply
because you told me to. i am now only a reflection of
your beliefs. i am no longer the person you once
desired to control. i am now the person you have
under your control.

majority

the level of fantasy to which i've grown accustomed to
has transcribed it's way into my heart.
often times i find myself wondering if i even know what
the word love means, if i know how it genuinely feels.
all because the supposed love i subject myself to makes
me despise love entirely.
so maybe i childishly wish that i have yet to know
genuine love.
as the "true love" i've felt
makes me never want to believe in love again.

tease

a cherry stem knot.
the art of tying the knot, comes through the tongue.
the skill it requires to hold the stem steady while artfully
and purposefully swirling ones tongue,
     all to achieve the perfect knot.
the practice itself is reminiscent of the art of lying.
the ability to produce a story, steady and strong, yet
sensually move ones tongue around the details they
wish to change.
tongues not only tie stems, but also creates art within
lies.

ugly

i never knew someone could embody so many opposite
personas
until, i came face to face
with all sides of you

damned

i've never been religious,
though i feel like i should've been.
as you've damned me to a life of pain.
and of hurt.
yet i have never been a sinner,
atleast not in the eyes of any lord.

competition

i entered a rigged competition with your love.
you loaded the gun, you set the pace.
you moved the finish line.
it was inevitable that i would fail.
but it still hurts nonetheless.

fire

loving you was like loving a piromaniac.
your love burned more than it healed,
yet it was so beautiful i never dared to let go.
because eventually the fire in my heart died
but the flames you left me,
made me believe i was still alight.

intoxication

my mother used to drink a lot when i was younger.
i never quite understood it other than when mom started
acting funny it was time to go to bed.
as i grew older, i contemplated sobriety,
toying with it as if it was a game.
however, i never knew what it was like to be drunk.
that is, until i found you.
and suddenly i understood why people become
intoxicated with things that weren't good for them.
i guess i am my mother after all.

blood

i watched you cut me.
i watched the blood spill over onto the floor.
i watched your smile as it happened.
and i wiped my blood up off the floor
and painted my face with a smile.
because even if our wounds weren't matching,
no one would ever know.

shards

you shattered my heart into jagged pieces.
i used all my strength to pick up the biggest one,
and i tried to shatter you too.
but the broken shard ripped through my grasp,
and left me on the ground,
hurting more than i did when you left.

bargaining

persistence

i leave my heart open for you everyday.
there's a neon sign outside it.
"come in and do what you want!
there's no repercussions!"
i'd never tell you i spend days afterwards picking up the
mess you made
because having you here, even painfully,
is better than not at all.
so i'll hang up my neon sign once again,
and await your return.

issues

i loved you despite your faults.
the scary things you said only pushed me to fight harder.
your issues were the reason i cared for you.
and mine were the reason you left.

maybe

if i had one word to describe my thoughts during our time together, it'd be "maybe". *maybe* if i gave you my body you'd love me more. *maybe* if i let you use me you'd stay a bit longer. *maybe* if i put my body through hell to look prettier, you would look at me instead of the other girls.
maybe maybe maybe.
maybe... one day i'd be enough for you.

seasonal

your love for me changed with the seasons.
we met in winter and fell in love in spring.
but by summer your eyes found someone else,
and in autumn i realized i was only second to.
then winter came back and you,
you were nowhere to be found.

reprimand

my heart craves revenge. it wants to level the playing field. to take you down to my level and make you understand my pain. but i can't even get an explanation. so i will settle for a sideways glance or a fleeting text. i will take what i can get and hope it's as painful for you as it is for me.

ideation

i created this version of you in my dreams. one where
you came back to me and said you were sorry. one
where you loved me and only me. where my body
and my heart alone were enough. i fell in love with
this dream.
and it broke my heart everytime i woke up.

fear

i am scared to live a life where i cannot love you openly.
one where i wake up and you're not my first text.
a life where i can't call your mom and ask what's for dinner,
or sit with you for hours and talk about our future kids.
i am terrified that this has become my reality.

competition

i watch who you choose to love nowadays.
and i can't stop comparing myself.
maybe if i looked like them, you'd still be here.
they are my competition in a game they're not even
aware they're playing.
pathetic isn't it?

lust

i give you access to my body
in hopes you'll lay with me for a moment after,
and i'll get to remember what it's like to be loved by you.
even momentarily.

mayhem

i'd upheave my life just to get another taste of your love.
i will ruin relationships with friends and family,
just to see you once again.
and have you love me like you used to
even if it's just for a moment.

indecisive

i let you toy with my heart because at the very least,
you're still touching me.
and i'd rather have part of you than none at all.
even if it kills me.
and even if i know i deserve better.

sparks

i hold your gaze as it burns into me. what was once your desire, is now only anger. the spark behind your eyes has turned to a blaze, spurting from your mouth like flames from a dragon. the hands to which i used to crave to hold, now burn in my grasp. they make me wonder, what did i used to crave from them at all?

wonder

i wonder what the attraction to toxicity really stems
from. is it a bad history? a lack of self respect? was
it the wrong place wrong time? the instances, the
reasons. all of the unexplained. whatever the root,
whatever the cause, it doesn't really matter. why
worry about where it came from? why not instead
worry about how to escape it?

maybe because it's easier to look back, than look forward
into the unknown.

want

i've never asked for much.
i don't demand expensive rings and flashy cars.
i pride myself on my humility.
yet as humble as i push myself to be,
there are still wants i have in my life.
and yet today, i cannot decide.
do i want you to stay? do i want to subject myself to
your hate?
or do i want to experience the euphoria of letting you go?
what do i want?

balance

to find a truth to be described as malleable,
to master the ways of deceit and balance,
holding ones' story while their tongue sinfully crafts it's
own reality.
though we envy those who hold the skill of tying cherry
stem knots,
we resent those whose artful tongue also crafts sins.

looking

gaze unto your lovers eyes and tell me what you see.
is it love?
lust?
anger?
hurt?
now look onto your own eyes.
does it mirror theirs?
do you hide your own to match them?
or have you noticed,
your eyes have changed?

worry

you called me crazy when i asked if there was anyone else.
you laughed when i told you my fears,
and i took that as reassurance.
i took your admittance of infidelity, as reassurance.
and i let myself be happy with it.

choose

i used to beg on my hands and knees.
me or them, *choose.*
and everytime you told me you chose me.
over and over and over again.
but you never did.
because give or take a week and we'd be right back where
we started.
their faces on your phone,
me on my knees,
and the tears that seem to be forever stained on my
cheeks.

scales

a relationship should be 50/50. an equally split load.
effort from both ends, a balancing act. but you
tipped the scales in your favor so that i gave
you everything with nothing to hide and you had
plenty of room for your secrets and lies.

requital

i wish i could get back the thousands of dollars i spent on
you. the hours i put into handmaking those cheesy gifts
for important anniversaries. the time and attention
from my days i spent on pleasing you. the parts of my
body i only let you touch. the smiles and kisses and
comfort we shared.
i wish i could get back the part of me that loved you.

division

my love was divided between fantasy and reality.
i often confuse the two.
as fantasy can be more enticing than reality
and reality can ruin whatever fantasy i conjured.
neither can exist without the other
but i wish this fantasy was my reality.

restlessness

you were fluid and i was stagnant.
i wanted you and only you.
you wanted someone else.
anyone else it seems.
whoever didn't look like me,
that was who you desired.

push

i gave you access to every part of me.
good or bad. pretty or ugly.
i hoped you'd love me anyway.
but when i tried to give you myself,
when i tried to love you,
it only pushed you away.

pull

i wish i could've pulled you in.
i wish the parts of me i gave you were enough.
my love and my time,
it should've kept you to me.
but your heart had no interest,
and your hands pulled me apart
and left me unwound.

bargaining

i surrender. i sit and lift my white flag in the air. watching as the wind swirls it's pathetic existence around my head, taunting me.

you can have your other lovers. i'll let you text who you want, watch what you desire. i will let myself be an option.

second best.

please, i will let you destroy me. i only ask to have you hold me and tell me you love me. give me some semblance

of normalcy. a fleeting smile here and there. a loving hand to hold.

i know i deserve more than half of you. but my heart loves all of you. so i'll take what i can get.

please, let me surrender.

depression

rain

i trace the raindrops that fall down the window pane like the tears i used to wipe from your face.
pretending that i'm making the sky feel better, wishing it was your heart i was tending to instead.
i'd like to think you're hurting too, that your heart has been ripped out and crushed to pieces.
that way when i look at my own, atleast then i'm not alone. even if you've left. and even if the rain is the only memory i have left of you.

hurt

i remember when i'd fall off my bike, and skin my knee.
how my mom would rush to my aide, scooping me up
with a band-aid and a kiss.
and how even when i was still bleeding, my tears
subsided.
and i felt okay.

my mom can no longer pick me up after i fall.
she picks up her wine glass and downs it in one.
i watch with shaking eyes as i have to pick her up off
the floor
and tend to her hurt.

when you came, i finally had someone to pick me up.
after i fell, and when i was laying on the floor hurt.
when my arms were tired from carrying everyone else,
you were there.

but just like her, you left.
you found some other way to cope, something to nurse.
and once again i sat shattered and alone.
picking up after another accident that was never mine to
begin with.

need

i needed you to survive.
i'd beg with my parents to let me drive to you.
through storms and floods,
i'd sit behind the wheel.
and i'd drive.
no matter the time, no matter the distance.
because the only thing that could save me,
the only person i needed,
was you.
but you never needed me.
and i haven't driven since.

pain

you watched as i carved your name onto my skin,
how i cried for you and begged for your love.
i put myself through hell all hoping to appease you.
to make you love me too.
but you enjoyed the pain more than the pleasure.

dissection

what is it about me?
everyone i've loved, everyone i gave my all too.
they all had someone else.
time after time again,
i'd find out the truth.
i wasn't anything to anyone.
my love meant jackshit.
but why? just- *why?*

disassociation

i became a ghost in our relationship.
after i found out the truth, when i learned you were
never just mine. when i saw how i'd never be
enough. i let myself love you still. but i was never
really there. i'd kiss your lips and tell you i loved
you, all while avoiding looking at your phone. i
would let you roam my body being sure to make
all the right noises at the right times, but i'd bury
my face in the pillows so you couldn't see the
tears falling. i let you hold me, i gave you access
to my body. but my soul had left.
for my head still wanted to love you,
but my heart was no longer in it.

mist

loving you was like being coated in a blanket of mist.
beautiful, peaceful, surrene.
leaving me completely unaware of the horrors that stood
right in front of me.

broken

my heart has begun to feel like a broken wine glass.
one that's been poorly put back together in an attempt
to hold wine once again.
in actuality, even if you pieced it together perfectly,
whispered all the right words and put all your care into it,
it's already been shattered.
and wine will forever weep from the cracks within the
fragmented glass.

tears

i knew i hated myself
when i made my favorite person cry.
to see my actions,
childish and immature,
create a river of tears that flow freely down their face.
i know in the moment leading up to the admittance,
i had already broken their heart.
but still,
their first single tear to fall,
well that broke my heart.
i cannot change it, i cannot take it back,
i cannot make it go away.
so why do i continue to be blessed their presence, one
with the heart of an angel,
when all i am is controlled by my demons?

(a letter i wish they'd write me)

void

i'm tired of staining my sheets red because i got tired of
drenching my clothes with tears.
i'm tired of loving people who only hurt me because i got
tired of hurting the people i love.
i'm tired of myself because i killed who i used to be in an
attempt to please everyone else,
yet all i did,
was kill myself entirely.

past

no one will ever know i'm upset just because i grabbed a
certain stuffed animal like you did,
yet no one will ever make me sad enough to grab it
like you.
no one will believe in me so much to make it to my dream
school like you did,
yet no one will undermine me like you.
no one will know my biggest dreams in life and the career
i'm killing myself for like you did,
yet no one will make me as scared of failure like you.
no one will ever love me as much as you did,
yet i hope no one will ever hurt me as much as you do.

trapped

the greens and blues that swim within her eyes glistened like the water belonging to a lake. she had the sweetest smile and the most contagious laugh. she carried so much potential, so many positives, it felt like a blessing to be able to be in her presence. i used to recognize her without a doubt. however, that girl went away long ago. life has been void of that lightness as it only seemed to follow her, never staying to hold her place. who would take away from such a beautiful creature? who would move this soul from the grasps of those who had fallen in love under her touch? her heart had sung with the voice of an angel and it's melody intertwined itself between the listeners ears and an inner desire to be one with her words. you could see colors and passion and emotion elicit from her lips as easily as water flows from the sky when the clouds become to heavy to carry it. the beauty- the joy. it carried her. it's funny though how quickly accidents change one. how one mistake, one day, one word. could completely shatter the world around. the person she was, the person who the world loved, was now broken. whisked away, never to be seen again. she tried to build back to the light she used to be. but his grasp, his hold, it shattered that dream. see, he saw her light, he fell for her touch. yet instead of falling under her smile as the world continued to do so, he fell sinister. he wanted that brightness, that temporal joy, only for himself. he went about his plan in the most wicked of ways. with snake eyes and a laced tongue, he held her within his grasp like an anaconda, squeezing the traits he desired so deeply, out of her. his words, his poison, kept her secluded only to him. her world had gone from reaching the ends of the earth, to the space he gave her between his fingers. he broke her. he took her and locked her away. broke her and beat her down. the lightness everyone craved to be under had been drained from her, feeding him and his twisted passion. he took that sunshine for himself and in the process, broke the person and happiness she supplied. she was no longer the sunshine of the room. she was a broken, scared little girl who was convincing herself she was okay. that she was doing the right thing. she tried to make it work, she tried to keep loving him, she tried to keep loving herself. but no matter her attempts, no matter her desire to escape, she was stuck. to this day, i cannot escape.

cold

you were my spark but time is a flame retardant

longing

falling to my knees, i cry out that i miss you.
i'd do anything for you to come home.
to love me again.
i wish you were here, and that you loved me too.
but my heart cries to an empty room,
where not even the echoes come back to me.

sickness

my doctor has given me a pile of prescriptions to take.
i reach my hand into the jar where i keep them,
grabbing a handful and hoping that they'll help for the
day.
it doesn't matter what i take or how many.
none of them will cure the pain you left me,
so i'll gamble anyway.

disappointment

"you weren't just a quick fuck" you promise me.
i repeat this to myself as you only answer my flirty texts.
i repeat this to myself when i only see my body staring
at me in our saved chat.
i repeat this to myself as i tell you i like you and you
go silent.
"you weren't just a quick fuck" i whisper to myself.

feelings

for years i kept a diary.
every hard day or trying conversation was recorded
within those pages.
i reread them when i couldn't find the strength to keep
going.
looking back on what i went through gave me motivation
to do it again.
but then you read those pages.
suddenly my own words became a weapon against myself.
and now they made an entirely different motivation.
one that would end, everything.

music

i like to drown my thoughts out with someone else's
pain, pretending i have someone who understands me.

alone

i don't fear being alone. in fact i quite enjoy it.
the whole world at my fingertips, on my own time.
but when i pass two people in love,
or a young family experiencing all their new firsts,
my heart grows heavy.
and suddenly, i no longer like being alone.

numb

"i'm so sorry. please forgive me"
my shattered heart takes your hands and with a shaking
voice, tells you it's okay.
we will get past this.
"i'm so sorry."
tears swim within my eyes as i wrap you in a hug and tell
you i understand.
there is still hope.
"i'm sorry."
i stand there with shaking fists and look you in your eyes
and whisper that it's okay.
everyone makes mistakes.
"sorry."
my head hangs low and i nod along to your words.
there's still a chance?
"..."
i sit on the floor of my shower, tongue dry and my head
empty.
i knew it was coming.

tissues

i find it funny how the only comfort i get is when i wipe
my face with a tissue.
i like to pretend it's your hands instead, brushing away
the hurt.
soaking up the pain that stains my face.
and that's why i smile to myself when i cry.
pure imagination.

demolition

i broke down every wall i had built around my heart
for you.
i convinced myself it was okay to love again.
and now i'm trying to remember what order i stacked
the bricks.

drowning

when a person drowns,
they thrash for air,
they fight the drag.
but something about drowning,
to me,
seems peaceful.
encased in something other than your thoughts.
you're too far below the surface to call out.
and it may burn,
but after the burn comes peace.
and that's what keeps me under.

heartbreak

i cast my love around like a hook on a reel,
putting myself in danger of loosing the bait.
simply to try to find a catch,
amongst an empty pond.

depression

weeds can grow through concrete.
they can break something larger than them.
thats how depression works.
it starts small,
simple.
until you're cracking at the seams.
and left with a broken heart.

acceptance

flower

finding a new flower
amongst the weeds of your life
excites you
you sprint towards it, eager to pick it and take it home
but you slow
you remember your past flowers
the excitement you got
the beauty it brought to your home when you brought
it in
but then
it wilted
because you became so fixated on watching it shine, you
uprooted it,
you forgot to water it
and soon enough, it wilted
and so when you meet this flower
and crouch beside it
you stop yourself
and instead of picking it up, with joy and excitement
you lie down beside it
and become entangled in its roots
so that you can always admire its beauty,
while making sure you keep it alive

change

change doesn't happen
if you dwell on those who keep putting you back
to square one

development

i dont want to be with someone
who doesnt make themselves better.
not for me, but for them

acceptance

when someone lets you go
sometimes, its better to relinquish your hold
than to try to tie the string back together

belief

you can't wait for someone to save you
you have to be the hero
to your own story

friend

a friend
gave me the world
holding my hand
and watching my heart
taught me so much more
than just what she was told
she taught me about space
and time
love
and galaxies
she gave me peace
in a world of war
even when life
beat her down
her frown never showed
her tears never fell
because she was strong
and smart
and she was loved
if only she knew how much

(she was me.)

lover

there is no lover in healing.
there is no one there to hold your hand or dry your tears.
you heal on your own.
only then, when you've mended your own heart,
with your own two hands.
can another lover come and share it's warmth.

health

we all take health for granted.
when we're sick, it's only then that we remember the
times of health.
when our noses were clear,
when we could breathe without coughing.
health also exists in our heart.
so as you go through heartbreak and pain,
that makes you forget what it's like to love freely,
learn to sit with that longing
and aide yourself back to health
so that you can experience love,
and not muddle in it's pain.

love

the best thing you can ever do
is let yourself love.
even if you're scared.
no-
especially if you're scared.

growth

becoming a new person,
surviving a heartbreak.
takes time.
it takes a nurturing hand and a patient soul.
after all, flowers don't bloom overnight.

future

i let myself sit in the remnants of the future we imagined together. and i let myself smile. i laugh at all the jokes we made and awe at how we thought our kids would look more like one of us than the other. i sigh in the dreamy moments we were going to have.
and then i take a deep breath and let it go. all with a smile on my face. because our future wasn't supposed to happen. and that's okay. just because our future doesn't exist doesn't mean i won't have one of my own.

flight

as a kid i used to dream of growing wings and being
able to fly,
soaring high above the clouds in a world of my own.
as i got older though, people told me it was impossible,
a childish dream i should let go of.
but that's not true at all.
as once you heal from a heartbreak,
once you let go of those prepercieved ideas of how life
was supposed to go,
only then do you realize you're soaring higher than you
ever thought you could.
despite it being "impossible"

beauty

you.
pure, naked, unfiltered you.
you my dear, are beautiful.
you always have been,
and always will, continue to be.

listen

learn to listen to yourself.
despite what anyone tells you.
you will always know yourself best.
and only you can save you when you need it most.

repaired

you will never be the same again after a heartbreak.
but that doesn't necessarily mean you're ruined.
after living through heartbreak after heartbreak,
i studied the art of kintsugi.
i learned how to fill the broken pieces of me with
something pure,
and learned to feel beautiful and whole
even with the cracks.

passion

find something to love that isn't another person. pour
your heart and soul into an activity that occupies
your thoughts and allows you to breathe. find a hobby.
give your love to something ordinary and you will
find that you can love yourself more, even if you're
only ordinary.

peace

i've learned to make peace with the pain.
i hold it's hand instead of running away.
it's almost become a friend of mine.
after all,
if it never leaves, why not learn to appreciate it?
it's much easier to live with a friend than an enemy.

clarity

there will never be a reason "why"
don't spend your life searching for answers that don't
exist.
live with the unknown.
let that become your clarity.

bloom

allow yourself to grow beyond the confines of your past.

rebirth

there is no redo to life.
undo buttons and backspaces do not exist.
don't focus on what could've been.
focus on what can be
and eventually it will be.
because you can always try again
even if you've already started.

light

the thing about your heart is it isn't a match.
it isn't lit once than fizzled out forever.
it's a floating ember from an eternal flame.
it may dwindle at times but will always remain alight.

dreams

it's okay to set your sights on something tangible and
close by to get you through the tough times.
dreams can be overrated anyways,
and that's okay.

content

before you can love yourself,
you must be okay with being content.
learning to be okay even on the days when you feel
unlovable,
that is the true measure of self-love.

interest

romanticize your life. skip as you walk to the grocery
store and smile at everyone on the way there. stop
to talk to the people sitting alone and take pictures
of the interesting plants you see. laugh at the
things that aren't remotely funny and post the
photos you'd normally delete.
be okay with being yourself.
unapologetically.

present

my heart still has days where it can't stand up by itself.
my eyes still cry myself to sleep sometimes and i sleep
through classes i was learning to enjoy. healing
doesn't mean perfection. it means getting to a place
where when your heart hurts and your head is
heavy. but, you let yourself rest. and you learn that
tomorrow will be okay.
but that today is an okay day to hurt as well.

you will be okay. even if it's not right now.

Author's Note

Thank you so much for reading my first ever published book! This book took years of my life to write. I went through heartbreak after heartbreak, learning and growing on the way. I hope you found some semblance of peace within my words and that you too will learn, it's okay to not be okay. And that there's always a promise of tomorrow, even if today is ruined.

I'd like to give my thanks to my friends and family who supported me through this journey. Everyone I've ever met has helped me finish this book and I wouldn't be here without them.

I love you all.

Hotlines

Help is always available. Don't wait until it's too late.

National Domestic Violence Hotline
1 (800) 799 - 7233 (SAFE)

National Suicide Hotline
988

National Sexual Assault Hotline
1 (800) 656 - 4673 (HOPE)

Self Injury Hotline
1 (800) 366 - 8288 (DONT-CUT)

Printed in the USA
CPSIA information can be obtained
at www.ICGtesting.com
LVHW011650240224
772712LV00065B/1759

Additional copies of *All Good People Go to Heaven and Other Religious Lore*
are available wherever good books are sold.

If you have enjoyed this book, or if it has had
an impact on your life,
we would like to hear from you.

Please contact us at:

HONOR BOOKS
Cook Communications Ministries, Dept. 201
4050 Lee Vance View
Colorado Springs, CO 80918

Or visit our Web site:
www.cookministries.com

HONOR ⊞ BOOKS
Inspiration and Motivation for the Seasons of Life

The Only Hell Is Here on Earth

In April 2005, rogue waves, some as high as seventy feet, crashed over the bow of a cruise ship. Ocean water cascaded down hallways and poured into cabins. Many passengers expected to die, but no one lost his life. Later, each passenger who was interviewed by the media related the horror of their brush with death. When asked whether they would take another cruise, each answered with one forceful word: "Never!"

If someone asked, "Do you want to go to hell?" how would you respond? Knowing that hell is a place of endless suffering and anguish, the only reasonable answer is, "Never!"